The Working White House

The Working White House

Text by
Haynes Johnson

Photographs by
Frank Johnston

A Washington Post Book

Praeger Publishers
New York

Published in the United States of America in 1975
by Praeger Publishers, Inc.
111 Fourth Avenue, New York, N.Y. 10003

© 1975 by Praeger Publishers, Inc.

Printed in the United States of America

Contents

PAGE

Preface   7

Some Working History   11

House and Home Today   55

For the Office of the President   81

Social Symbol   129

Acknowledgments   183

Photo Credits   185

Preface

For 175 years, from the time of John Adams, the White House has been home for American Presidents. It has sheltered them in their private moments alone with their families and served them in their public roles as leaders of the Western world. Over the decades the White House has been something more. It is the people's house, visited and treasured by millions of Americans and by guests from other lands.

The stories of the Presidents who have lived and worked in this house have been told often and in many ways. From the earliest days of the Republic to the present, administration after administration, artists have sketched the symbolic White House and photographers have captured it on film. Its ceremonial rooms, particularly the Oval Office, where the President works and receives his visitors, are familiar to Americans.

But there remains an untold story, an unseen White House peopled by those largely anonymous men and women who over the years have worked unceasingly behind the scenes to make the Executive Mansion function—

as home, as office, as symbol—day and night, winter and summer, in crisis and in tranquility. Some of these people tend the grounds, change the beds, wash the linens and the dishes, scrub and polish the floors, dust and refurbish the treasured objects that have been used, many of them, by the thirty-six Presidents who have lived there up to now. Other White House workers sort the mail, protect the President, serve the press as it covers the President's business, and supervise the great state dinners at which distinguished guests see the house on those splendid social occasions that help set the tone for the nation and provide the setting in which much business gets done.

In photographs and text, this book shows how the White House is managed today and tells something about how its routine came to be established. It is the story of the working White House.

The
Working
White
House

Photo by Mathew Brady, 1861

Some Working History

Major Pierre Charles L'Enfant stood on the highest point of ground, gazing out over the woods and marshes toward the distant low-lying hills. He was a visionary, irascible, vain, touched with genius. Out of the wilderness stretching for miles before him he would create a monumental federal city, ten miles square, diamond-shaped, with grand, wide avenues and stately buildings, a suitable symbol for the promise of a struggling young republic. In the very center of his diamond he would place the most magnificent structure of all—a "President's House" that, as he envisioned it, would have "the sumptuousness of a palace . . . and the agreeableness of a country seat."

It was no palace that was built along the Potomac, and for years there was little that was agreeable about either the big house constructed of sandstone or the city in which it was located. Washington for a long time remained a dismal village, crude, unsanitary, and uncomfortable. Parts of it still are. In time the White House fulfilled L'Enfant's dream. It became at once simple and grand, ceremonial and informal, private living quarters and public business office, treasured museum and world center of decisions on war and peace. But it did not begin that way, and for years it bore no resemblance to the smoothly functioning, working White House of the present.

When John Adams, the first of the Presidents to live in the White House, took occupancy in 1800, he found a dark, damp, unfinished mansion, lacking the most basic essentials. Plaster and paint were still wet. There was not even enough firewood to heat the home. "Not one room or chamber is finished of the whole," his wife, Abigail, wrote. "To assist us in this great castle, and render less attendance necessary, bells are wholly wanting—promises are all you can obtain."

As the first mistress of the President's House, Abigail Adams had to go to Congress to lobby for firewood. Not until two weeks after she and her husband moved in did Congress authorize the hiring of a workman. James Clarke built a staircase for them and put a window in the East Room. He also built a privy for the First Family.

When Abigail, as hardy as she was determined, discovered no place had been prepared to hang the White House wash outside, she ordered the servants to use the cavernous East Room. There, where so much history would be made, where President's bodies would lie in state and their daughters would be wed, the sheets and towels and the President's underwear were strung out to dry.

The White House, like the nation, grew slowly and painfully. Each presidential family left a legacy to the next, and to the country they each in turn represented. The Adamses established the dignified, formal tone of entertaining that would become the custom for succeeding administrations. Each week they greeted guests upstairs in the Oval Room, which in time they filled with mahogany chairs and sofas upholstered in crimson damask. Today John Adams's words, carved on the mantel of the State Dining Room, remind us of a letter he wrote his wife after his first night in the White House. "I pray heaven to bestow the best of Blessings on this House and all that hereafter inhabit it," he wrote. "May none but honest and wise men ever rule under this roof."

Thomas Jefferson, the Virginia country gentleman who had so enjoyed his days as the American Minister to France, dressed, ate, and lived simply himself. But to run the White House he employed Etienne Lemaire, a French steward. The staff included a French chef and a dozen of Jefferson's own personal servants from Monticello. And at his table he served delicacies imported from Europe, the best vintages from France, Spain, Italy, and Portugal. It was Jefferson who began to add the touches of grandeur that would become associated with the White House. A noted architect himself (he had submitted an anonymous plan for the original White House construction competition in 1792 under the letters "A.Z."), he hired Benjamin Latrobe, the most famous American architect of the day, to assist him in adding to the mansion. Using his own Virginia home of Monticello as a model, he built terraces and pavilions, servants' quarters, a wine cellar for those vintage bottles, a stable, a laundry, and ice, meat, and chicken houses. He left behind him his plans for the White House porticos, finally built in Andrew Jackson's day, now so distinctive a feature of the structure.

Jefferson's trappings of splendor were not always appreciated by his fellow citizens. The Executive Mansion, a newspaper of the day commented acidly, was already "big enough for two emperors, one pope, and the grand lama."

It was not until Dolley Madison began her tenure as First Lady, however, that the White House entered a period of grace and gaiety. Under the energetic direction of Dolley, the first great Washington hostess, the White House became the scene of a whirl of dances, teas, lawn and dinner parties that made the Executive Mansion the social center of the nation. The mighty of the land attended her celebrated Wednesday night "drawing room" affairs. One of her guests, Washington Irving, penned a description of Dolley that has endured: "Mrs. Madison is a fine, portly, buxom dame who has a smile and a pleasant word for everybody."

When the British captured Washington and burned the city in Dolley

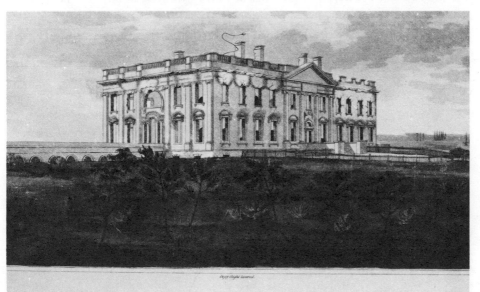

A VIEW of the PRESIDENTS HOUSE in the CITY of WASHINGTON after the Conflagration of the 24th August 1814.

and James Madison's time, the house became a blackened, burnt-out, roofless, hollow shell. Only its stately outer walls remained standing.

For three years there was no President's House. Its reconstruction proceeded slowly and laboriously. At times it seemed as if the work never would be completed. Madison was succeeded by James Monroe. Under intensive prodding from James Hoban, the Irishman from Charleston who had been the original White House architect and was also in charge of its rebuilding, the work pace was accelerated. On New Year's Day, 1818, the house once more was opened to the public at a reception given by the Monroes.

"The President's House, for the first time since its reaerification, was thrown open for the general reception of visitors," a Washington newspaper reported. "It was thronged from 12 to 3 o'clock. . . . It was gratifying once more to be able to salute the President of the United States with the compliments of the season in his appropriate residence."

The long wait had been worthwhile. For the first time the mansion bore a gleaming coat of the fresh white paint that has since become its most notable feature.

Inside, the new White House bore a look of formal elegance. Monroe himself, who like Jefferson and John and Abigail Adams had been influenced by the French style, contributed a number of his own exquisite furnishings for use in two bedrooms, the State Dining Room, and the drawing rooms.

From Paris he ordered other furniture and decorative objects. His silver-gilt flatware, including a set of gold-plated spoons, became the model for dining utensils used in the White House ever since. Entertaining again was formal and elaborate. Yet the White House still retained an open, informal air. A newspaper account sketched this scene of a public reception:

The secretaries, senators, foreign ministers, consuls, auditors, accountants, officers of the army and navy of every grade, farmers, merchants, parsons, priests, lawyers, judges, auctioneers and nothingarians—all with their wives and some with their gawky offspring, crowd to the President's house every Wednesday evening; some in shoes, most in boots and many in spurs; some snuffing, others chewing, and many longing for their cigars and whiskey-punch left at home; some with powdered heads, others frizzled and oiled, whose heads a comb has never touched, and which are half-hid by dirty collars (reaching far above their ears) as stiff as pasteboard.

The President's House was still the people's home.

The intellectual and moody John Quincy Adams, despite his sophistication and tastes acquired during his own service for America abroad, made no major physical changes in the White House, and under him it was run rather stiffly, though one great and very emotional social event occurred during his tenure.

General Lafayette, on his last visit to the United States, lived at the White House as a guest of the Adamses during the summer of 1825. (He apparently was something of an eccentric: He left a live alligator in the East Room until a proper place to keep it was found, and he also strewed gifts he received all over the sofas, chairs, and floor.) On the day before Lafayette left for France, the President gave a formal farewell. The White House was jammed with invited guests who came to pay tribute. The general was so moved that he broke down and wept. After Adams had praised him lavishly in a speech, Lafayette responded with the words "God bless the American people, each of their states, and the Federal Government." Then he embraced Adams emotionally. Tears ran down the cheeks of both men.

Andrew Jackson, the people's President with the supposedly rough-hewn frontier tastes, saw that the White House was finished structurally in the style now familiar to the world. Jackson immediately began work on the twelve-column North Portico, using Latrobe's design from 1807. It was completed in 1830, and has been used as the ceremonial entrance to the White House ever since.

Jackson also transformed the interior of the White House, spending on it what were then vast sums of money. Three cut-glass chandeliers, each holding eighteen candles, rich draperies, a Brussels carpet, tables topped with the finest Italian marble, vases, sconces, reupholstered furniture, a large and elegant French silver service, splendid china and glassware—all were added during his time in office. More important, he saw to it that the White House finally had a more basic necessity, running water.

When John and Abigail Adams first had moved into the White House, the nearest usable water supply was half a mile away. Servants brought them their water daily from Franklin Park. It wasn't until 1833, under Jackson, that spring water was piped into the White House.

For all the elegance of his presidency, Jackson did not neglect the common touch that so endeared him to his fellow citizens. From his tumultuous inauguration day when he threw open the White House for the people (and created a legend as the mob crammed into the mansion, standing on furniture in muddy boots, fighting, crawling through windows, breaking china, and leaving a shambles in their wake) Jackson continued to draw the populace inside his, and its, home. His last public reception was memorable—and odorous. On Washington's Birthday, in 1837, he once more threw open the doors of the White House for the people. A monstrous cheese that had been sent to him by a New York State dairy-man was placed inside the vestibule. The public was invited to help itself of the enormous offering, which weighed 1,400 pounds and was four feet high and two feet wide. The people did so with relish. They tore into the cheese with knives and fingers and demolished it. "The company reminded one of Noah's Ark—all sorts of animals, clean and unclean," one person who was present wrote afterward. The smell of Jackson's cheese lingered for days (some, unkindly, said for years).

After Jackson's administration, improvements to the President's House were added gradually—the grand landscape design for the eighteen-acre estate in 1851, central heating in 1853, a bath in 1855, the greenhouse in 1857, telephones in 1877, an elevator in the 1880s, electric lights in 1889, a new Executive Wing connected to the house by a colonnade and a small white office building in the early 1900s under Theodore Roosevelt, and the East Wing in the 1930s under Franklin Roosevelt. The final physical stage of the modern White House was completed during Harry S. Truman's administration.

By the time Truman became President, in 1945, the White House had grown haphazardly and, as it turned out, dangerously. For years it was common knowledge that the building was in sad condition. It looked far more sound than it was. When large functions were held in the East

Room, for instance, heavy pilings had to be placed under the floor for protection. Then more ominous evidence was detected: A chandelier in the East Room swung erratically during a party, a leg of Margaret Truman's piano crashed through the upstairs floor, a bathtub used by President Truman himself came close to falling through. A committee of architects and engineers examined the White House and reported back their gloomy findings to Truman. The building was in imminent danger of collapse. Walls were crumbling, plaster was cracked, beams were split, and the entire building rested on soft clay in footings only eight feet deep. The Trumans evacuated the President's House and moved into Blair House across the street.

From 1948 to 1952, at a cost of some $5.5 million, the entire interior of the White House was removed, and carefully stored. None of the old interior wall and ceiling decorations could be saved. Instead, plaster garlands, shields, cornucopias, and elaborate bas–reliefs were painstakingly copied. As bulldozers excavated for a two-story basement, and construction crews erected a new foundation and steel framework inside the old walls, reminders of the house's history were uncovered before the workmen's eyes: an old well from the Jefferson presidency, stones, still blackened, from the Madison tenure during the War of 1812, and a corridor ceiling done in gold leaf from the days of the Monroes.

Truman added a personal touch. He asked Congress to provide money for a balcony behind the massive pillars of the South Portico. Although it was a subject of some controversy at the time, the President got his wish. The balcony was built; it will always be known as the Truman balcony.

The changes that have occurred at the White House as each President and First Lady added their own stamp have been more than architectural and decorative. They have also had to do with staffing and management.

When the lion of English literature, as Charles Dickens was known in the cliché of his time, came to America for the first time in 1842, his travels led him inevitably to Washington. There he approached the Executive Mansion bearing an official invitation from the President and accompanied by a distinguished member of the government. Casually strolling up to the front entrance, he entered a large hall and rang a bell. Once. Twice. Three times. No one answered. Dickens walked on through room after room on the ground floor. There were men standing idly, their hats on, their hands in their pockets. Others lounged on the chairs and sofas, while still others lay about listlessly, yawning drearily.

Dickens continued on. Upstairs, in a drawing room, he found other visitors awaiting audiences with the President. He noticed a black servant in plain clothes and yellow slippers gliding noiselessly about, whispering messages in the ears of the more impatient visitors, and then gliding off again.

Nearby he inspected another chamber. It was dominated by a great bare wooden desk on which piles of newspapers had been placed. Surrounding the desk was a sight that made Dickens blanch:

There were some fifteen or twenty persons in the room. One, a tall, wiry, muscular old man, from the west; sunburnt and swarthy; with a brown white hat on his knees, and a giant umbrella resting between his legs; who sat bolt upright in his chair, frowning steadily at the carpet, and twitching the hard lines about his mouth, as if he had made up his mind "to fix" the President on what he had to say, and wouldn't bate him a grain. Another, a Kentucky farmer, six feet six in height, with his hat on, and his hands under his coat-tails, who leaned against the wall and kicked the floor with his heel, as though he had Time's head under his shoe, and were literally "killing" him. A third, an oval-faced, bilious-looking man, with sleek black hair cropped close, and whiskers and beard shaved down to blue dots, who sucked the head of a thick stick, and from time to time took it out of his mouth, to see how it was getting on. A fourth did nothing but whistle.

What most upset Dickens was the behavior of all these assorted Americans in their President's House. They all kept spitting upon the carpet. They were, he noted, so very persevering and so very energetic in their abundant spitting "that I take it for granted the Presidential housemaids have high wages, or, to speak more genteelly, an ample amount of 'compensation:' which is the American word for salary, in the case of all public servants."

1, President Jackson's Kitchen. 2, Hugo Ziemann, Steward of the Presidential Household.

WASHINGTON, D.C. — THE WHITE HOUSE KITCHEN — PREPARING DINNER.

FROM A SKETCH BY C. BUNNELL. — SEE PAGE 143.

Dickens would have been saddened to learn of the status of most White House servants. They were not well paid. Indeed, until the Civil War many of them received no "compensation." They were slaves. What paid staff there were received only paltry remuneration. Their financial rewards came not from a grateful nation and its elected representatives in Congress; the President himself had to pay all the wages of his servants, as well as all expenses for running the Executive Mansion. That included paying for all official entertaining. Even the wealthiest of Presidents found it a virtual impossibility to maintain the style expected of the nation's leader. Jefferson and Monroe had to sell land to pay off debts from their presidential years. The result was a casual, careless air about the White House for more than a century. The public saw only the surface grace and glitter; behind the scenes the lovely house was a burden to run and a shambles.

21

This state of affairs continued up to the administration of William Howard Taft in 1909. Not until then did Congress vote funds to pay for the President's servants. And it wasn't until Warren G. Harding's time in the early 1920s that Congress appropriated money to help defray the cost of official presidential entertaining. Until the twentieth century there hadn't even been a woman housekeeper in over-all charge of supplying the presidential family's daily needs. Marketing was so casual that at least one President sometimes did his own grocery shopping. It was not uncommon to see the small figure of William Henry Harrison carrying home his groceries in a market basket.

The story is told, apparently truthfully, of Franklin Pierce's inaugural experience. Cheered by the crowds massed in the Capitol Plaza as he gave his first presidential address, hailed along the route of the Presidents as he made his way into his new home, and surrounded by the hordes of well-wishers inside the mansion that night for the formal festivities, Pierce finally found himself alone. Throughout the White House were piles of dirty dishes and disarranged furniture. There was no one to clean up the mess. What servants there were had disappeared, and the new President of the United States had to grope his way upstairs by candlelight to begin his tenure in office.

The small domestic staff of the White House in May 1877, during Rutherford B. Hayes's administration.

The working White House generally belied its splendid outward public appearance. The domestic areas were far from grand. When Irwin Hood (Ike) Hoover first reported to work at the White House in 1891 during Benjamin Harrison's administration, he was staggered by what he saw. Hoover, who was to serve as chief usher for nine Presidents, recalled his first tour of the mansion:

While waiting for definite orders, I looked around in what was then the basement. The floor was covered with damp and slimy brick; dust webs were everywhere. An old wooden heating trough hung the entire length of the ceiling of the long corridor. Everything was black and dirty. Rooms that are now parlors were then used for storage of wood and coal. In the kitchen of the original house, now an engine room, could be seen the old open fireplaces once used for broiling the chickens and baking the hoecakes for the early Fathers of our country, the old cranes and spits still in place. Out of the door to the rear there yet remained the old wine-vault, the meathouse, and the smokehouse. So vivid were these reminders you could still almost smell the wine odors and the aromas from the hams and bacon that must have been so deliciously and painstakingly prepared there.

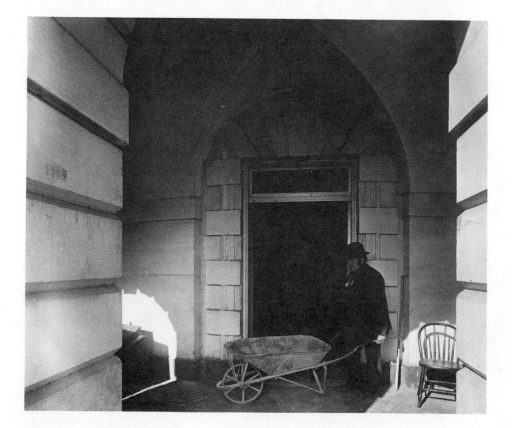

Everything about the working White House then was casual. The entire housekeeping office totaled only ten people, and four of those were doorkeepers and messengers. Security was unbelievably lax. Only three policemen and one watchman were assigned to patrol the outside grounds around the White House. One night, when President Harrison was sitting on the south porch, a drunken stranger jumped over the iron fence and came directly up to the President without being halted or even detected. Inside, the kitchen was in deplorable condition. Floors in many parts of the mansion consisted of dirty, moldy bricks. There was only one bathroom in the entire building. Servants, of whom there were no more than six, continued to work with antiquated implements. Old Jerry, a black janitor, swept the floors with a feather duster. Other men just as simply cut grass, shoveled snow, delivered messages, grew lilies, and guarded gates. Still others charted war moves, typed correspondence, sent telegrams, handled incoming mail, and contemplated problems of security.

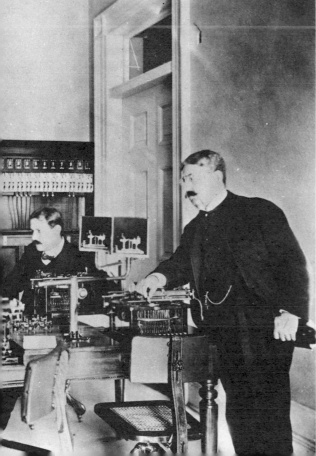

Only after President William Howard Taft was authorized to hire a housekeeper and general manager for the White House was the mansion put on a professionally managed basis. Before then the principal White House duties had been handled by a steward, who in turn would call in caterers for the major social events. Under the Tafts this ancient practice was discarded. From then on the White House was run as a home, albeit an extraordinary one, where a heavy schedule of the most demanding entertaining was mandatory.

Elizabeth Jaffrey, the first housekeeper and general manager, began to do her own marketing, traveling to the various Washington establishments in a horse-drawn carriage. That custom was continued until 1926. She bought in large quantities—butter by the tub, potatoes by the barrel, fruit and fresh vegetables by the crate.

"Throughout all my seventeen and a half years at the White House," she wrote later, "my daily program remained practically the same. I would have a short conference with the President's wife in the morning after I had studied the day's social calendar and worked out the menus with the cook. Food was only a small part of this conference; there would be the endless problem of keeping the whole White House in order—the servants, the linen, the silver, the furniture, the decorations and furnishings, and a thousand and one other details."

As only one indication of the primitive conditions then in vogue at the White House, all the wash was done every day by hand. Before the Tafts as many as nine women had been employed to do the immense amount of laundry. After they entered the White House, the laundry staff was cut from nine to three. How they managed, or if they really did, is a fact lost to history.

In Mrs. Jaffrey's day—she served until 1926—there were twenty-seven White House staff employees. Their duties were rigidly laid out; they were assigned to specific tasks broken down into four categories. Below stairs were the head cook, with two assistants; a kitchen helper; three laundresses; a housemaid; a head mechanic; an electrician; and one man in charge of the furnace during the day and another at night. On the first floor were four footmen assigned to each door, and one parlor maid. For the dining rooms and pantry there were a head butler and his assistant and a pantry man. Upstairs, in the family quarters, there were four maids, a houseman, and a special valet.

As Mrs. Jaffrey and subsequent White House overseers quickly learned, these staff members had settled themselves into distinct and separate castes. The four or five senior male servants dined at a table by themselves. The dining room staff would gather in the pantry to eat what was left over from the President's own table. A third group, consisting of the laundresses and charwomen, ate at yet another table by themselves.

When this old status system was abolished, there was sharp dissatisfaction. It grew so bad that only the threat of dismissal ended an incipient staff revolt.

But custom and tradition die hard at the White House.

When Henrietta Nesbitt came to the White House to begin nearly thirteen years' service as chief housekeeper for Franklin and Eleanor Roosevelt, she immediately encountered the heavy hand of tradition.

"The doorman took my coat with the big fur collar and hung it over a nail in the hall rack," she recalled, "and the nail went right through the fur!

"I made a mental note to get rid of those nails. But I never did. I would succeed in ridding the White House of cuspidors, feather dusters, and corn brooms, but I never did banish the nails. They were traditional, like so many other things. So I ran my neck into tradition my first minute in the White House, and it was the start of a struggle that would last thirteen years. Sometimes I won, but tradition won most of the time."

Even more depressing was her sight of the White House kitchen. Her heart sank.

"This was the 'first kitchen in America,' and it wasn't even sanitary. Mrs. Roosevelt and I poked around, opening doors and expecting hinges to fall off and things to fly out."

They found dark-looking cupboards, a huge old-fashioned range, sinks with time-worn wooden drains, and a rust-marked wooden dumbwaiter. The refrigerator was also wooden. And it smelled bad. The electric wiring was old and dangerous.

"This," she said, "was a great big wonderful old house, and it was almost empty of the necessities."

As housekeeper, Mrs. Nesbitt was charged with overseeing the maintenance of sixty rooms and twenty baths. It was an immense task. She quickly learned that each of the four floors was like a home in itself, and each had a life and history of its own. Every piece of furniture had its own tradition to be kept up.

For years a special schedule was followed just to handle the cleaning of the immense chandeliers in the East Room. White House carpenters built trestles under the chandeliers for workmen to stand on while they dusted each of the twenty-two thousand separate pieces of glass. They removed the glass prisms, one at a time, washed them with alcohol, polished them, and hung them back in place. This job was done once a year, just before the formal social season began. Six men worked a day and a half merely to do the polishing. The entire job took them a full week to finish.

Because of the heavy crush of tourists flocking through the building (a million a year during FDR's administration, a figure that doubled by the mid-1970s), simply keeping the building clean was a major, and endless, undertaking. Early each morning in the 1930s and 1940s the ground floor was scrubbed. Throughout the day it was mopped up as required. All the linen covers on the chairs had to be changed each day. One man was assigned to take care of the Grand Staircase alone. It was dusted three or four times daily. Starting at the top of the stairs a man dusted his way down to the bottom—and then began working his way up once more.

While all this was going on painters, carpenters, electricians, and plumbers were kept constantly at work.

Platoons of other employees took care of washing the 160 windows, skylights, and mirrors, dusting paintings and furniture, polishing the brasswork and silver, cleaning the hearths, putting out flowers daily throughout the mansion.

A set of rules promulgated during the Franklin Roosevelt administration offers a fascinating glimpse into only one aspect of what it was like to maintain the White House then:

RULES GOVERNING HOUSEMAIDS AND HOUSEMEN

1. In the morning, the maids make up the beds using the same linen, if the guests are staying more than the night. They put fresh water in the rooms, clean the ash trays and silver, so the men can follow immediately to do their work. After the men are through, the maids dust the rooms and finish all the little extra things such as pins, stationery, soap, towels, etc., seeing everything is in perfect order. As soon as the rooms are completed, the maids are to retire to the third floor, leaving the second floor

for guests only. The maids should be ready to answer any bells when they are rung. All spare time is to be spent in helping with the mending.

2. When the house is being put in order for special occasions, no one is supposed to leave until everything is in order and ready, regardless of time.

3. The men and maids must come upstairs when their lunch hour is over, while the family and guests are at their meals, and have everything tidied up by the time the people return to their rooms.

4. The men must keep the closet clean, next Miss Thompson's office, being sure it is left clean every day.

5. The men must help each other to take up and down the laundry.

6. The help must not engage guests in conversation. Only speak when spoken to, unless it is regarding the guest's clothes.

7. When the guests and family go to dinner, the maids put the fruit in the rooms and take out the flowers, tidy up the ash trays, and dust.

8. Maids must not put linen with holes, or torn linen, in the bathrooms or on the beds.

9. Each one should let the head man know when he is leaving the building for an errand, or wants to get off.

10. After the cleaning up after lunch, maids dress for the P.M. The maids must be dressed and at their posts when the guests arrive, if there are ladies coming.

11. The men must look out for the luggage. The men and the maids both unpack if the people wish it.

12. The third-floor man must help to clean the brass from the second floor.

13. The maids are to give assistance when inventory is taken of linen for the second and third floors.

In those days, tradition still dictated many of the customs. Indeed, they still do. In the East Room, where the formal state receptions were held, the four fireplaces were all carefully laid according to old custom: paper, kindling, heavy wood, and then large logs. All well seasoned, of course. No smoldering or smoking fires in the White House.

The job of making the White House work fell on ushers, secretaries, maids, valets, doormen, butlers, chambermaids, engineers, maintenance men, gardeners, groundskeepers, drivers, aides, and communications specialists, to name only some of those responsible. The public saw only the smoothly functioning official residence of the President—the receptions for as many as two thousand people under FDR, the balls and state dinners, the presidential addresses and conferences.

Behind the scenes at the White House, though, were problems common to ordinary homes, but hardly associated with the formal grandeur of the nation's most exquisite residence. Until the Truman White House restoration was completed in 1952, there was a perpetual battle with black ants. It was a war that went on continuously, even during official functions. The ants appeared everywhere, sometimes in great swarms.

And there were cockroaches in the kitchen, buffalo moths in the furniture storerooms, mice upstairs and down and, more serious, an ancient White House problem—rats. During Theodore Roosevelt's time, the rats were still a menace. They tunneled into the home from the outside. No matter how hard the gardeners, and later the exterminators, tried to eliminate them, the rats still found a way inside the White House.

(Even in 1975, after all the rebuilding and refinishing of the old home, people who work late in their offices will say they are often disturbed by the sound of something running through the walls. Could there still be rats in the White House?)

The job of maintenance has never been the only one confronting the staff. As in any large household, there have been inevitable tensions and frictions among the employees themselves and with the presidential families they served. The delicate problems of caste and class that Mrs. Jaffrey encountered among the kitchen staff in the Taft era no doubt existed earlier and have had their sequels in later administrations. A certain cook working in the Eleanor and Franklin Roosevelt White House had undeniable talents but an abrasive and temperamental personality. For years she created problems, but the Roosevelts were reluctant to dismiss her. "We have to treat her like a child," Mrs. Roosevelt would say when told of another unpleasant episode. The situation did not improve.

"Many a dish was spoiled," Henrietta Nesbitt remembered long after leaving the White House herself, "thanks to her having a sulking spell, into the third administration. She played havoc throughout the first two, but the President was patient, until she began sending up too many dishes he didn't like, and that was the end, even for anyone as forgiving as Mrs. Roosevelt."

The cook was transferred.

Much later, during Lyndon Johnson's presidency, the public did learn of another internal bit of White House employee temperament. René Verdon, the White House chef, abruptly resigned. Ostensibly his resignation was prompted by his being asked to prepare dishes for the White House table out of a cookbook. French chefs don't read cookbooks. They write them.

A French journalist offered a darker interpretation of this grave step. "The worst can be feared from a man who has red snapper served with a salad of beets and cream, as was the case for President Johnson," he wrote in Paris. "Chef René Verdon held in his hands the stomach on which the peace of the world depends. It is understandable that he recoiled before so much responsibility."

Despite such tempests, which have marked every administration, it has even been possible for romance to flourish unnoticed among the presidential staff. In 1971, during Richard Nixon's first administration, Heinz Bender, a White House pastry chef, and Shirley Bailey, the mansion's housekeeper, were married secretly. Their romance had grown slowly over a nineteen-month period. They were married immediately after the Nixons had left to begin a summer vacation in California. "It was a deep secret," Bender said later. "I didn't even bake a cake."

Working at the White House is never easy. Not only must the employees do their jobs quickly and efficiently. They must accomplish them in something resembling a self-effacing state. Their tasks must never interfere with the President's functions or detract from the appearance of the White House itself. Although their work is best if it is hardly noticed by anyone, they labor in a home that the entire world is watching. This

is difficult enough. But working at the White House also means facing a constant fact of life not found in any other job in any other home: Everyone there is aware that at any moment of night or day presidential power can pass suddenly, sometimes nightmarishly, from one hand to another. And the immediate burden of keeping the White House working falls on all of those who labor there.

On nine occasions the White House has seen the President suddenly taken before he completed his term. Four of the Presidents were murdered —Lincoln, Garfield, McKinley, Kennedy. Four died of disease while in office—Harrison, Taylor, Harding, Franklin Roosevelt. Nixon resigned abruptly in the face of impeachment proceedings. Each of these occasions precipitated a national crisis. Each time the White House staff helped to make it possible for the new President to seize the reigns of power immediately and smoothly.

Not only in such traumatic transfers of presidential power are White House workers taxed severely. Even when the transition is the normal and expected outcome of an election that puts a new President in office, they face subtle challenges, new demands and requirements. Each presidential occupant requires new standards of taste and style. Each sets a tone distinctly different from his predecessors'. Each creates new problems for the working White House. The employees, many of whom have worked at the White House for a lifetime, must be prepared to adapt immediately to the constantly changing styles of administration after administration.

Theodore Roosevelt's zest in his personal life and formality in his public functions gave way to William Howard Taft's often fractious nature. Woodrow Wilson's ascetic life-style was replaced by Warren G. Harding's conviviality and poker parties. Calvin Coolidge's eccentricities and stinginess led into Herbert Hoover's era of lavish entertaining and formal style. Franklin Roosevelt's exuberant air of casual disorder was followed by Harry Truman's simple manner. Dwight Eisenhower's military method of operating through a carefully delineated command structure was supplanted by the youthful dash of John Kennedy's thousand days. Lyndon Johnson's attention to detail and overwhelming personality swiftly were replaced by Richard Nixon's moodiness and habit of seclusion. Gerald Ford's White House again reflected the personality of the President: open, freer, less tense and driven, marked by good humor and spirits.

The public sensed these aspects of life in the White House, but rarely saw the side that the employees had to confront. Each President and First Lady wanted their guests to be housed in a certain fashion, their meals to be prepared differently, their living arrangements changed, their office schedules and methods of governing revamped.

(Top) William McKinley, twenty-fifth President, dictates to his secretary in his somber office. McKinley's successor, Teddy Roosevelt, set a much livelier pace, and his children also contributed to the spirit of the times. (Bottom) Archie Roosevelt and his younger brother Quentin join the White House police for roll call and inspection.

(Opposite, top) Woodrow Wilson talks to an Army pilot over a wireless telephone from the White House grounds. (Bottom) Franklin D. Roosevelt meets the press. (Above) Secret Service men accompany Harry Truman on his morning stroll to the executive offices in the White House.

Chief executives and their wives required special handling, often over the smallest personal matters. Franklin Roosevelt once upbraided Henrietta Nesbitt. "Mrs. Nesbitt," the President said firmly, "I like my cream in lobs and gobs." Mrs. Nesbitt had been doing her best, but was nevertheless unsuccessful. No matter how many farms she personally investigated in Maryland and Virginia, she could not match the quality of cream produced by FDR's Hyde Park cows—at least in the President's mind.

Bess Truman, Harry's wife, was beloved by the White House employees, but she had a reputation of being a morning grouch. Privately, the butlers would speculate among themselves about the state of her daily morning mood. "Is she wearing two guns this morning?" the head butler asked another who was serving Mrs. Truman breakfast one morning.

Mamie Eisenhower, despite her girlish manners, could be autocratic in ordering the staff. One day President Eisenhower asked to see the menu for a luncheon he was giving. The menu came back with a handwritten notation: "Approved DDE."

Mrs. Eisenhower happened to spot the menu. "What's this?" she asked. "I didn't approve this menu!"

J. B. West, chief usher at the White House, explained that the President had approved the menu two or three days earlier.

Mrs. Eisenhower shook her head in annoyance.

"I run everything in my house," she said. "In the future all menus are to be approved by *me* and not by anybody else!"

Another time Mrs. Eisenhower started to get in an elevator and was angered to see it go right past her carrying a house employee.

"Never use my elevator again!" she commanded.

Jacqueline Kennedy threw the staff into a state of shock with all the changes she began making in the White House. "I can't believe what they're doing," a housekeeper said to J. B. West.

Mrs. Kennedy also asked West if a colonnade leading to the swimming pool (later taken out of use during Nixon's tenure) could be enclosed in glass, similar to the east entrance. Her reason: She wanted the President to be able to walk back from the swimming pool without being exposed to cold air. Kennedy swam in the nude, a practice favored by Lyndon Johnson.

The change was not made. As West said in his memoir, *Upstairs at the White House*, written with Mary Lynn Kotz, he couldn't see "changing that stately colonnade for one President's pleasure."

Lyndon Johnson's impress was felt immediately. On his first night in the White House he bounded forth from the king-sized four-poster in which John Kennedy had slept to question chief usher West. Waving his arms and pointing into the halls, he demanded to know who paid

Eleanor Roosevelt works at her desk with her personal secretary, Marvella Thompson (seated), and her social secretary, Edith Helm.

(Opposite, top) Mamie Eisenhower goes over White House menus with John Ficklin in the White House kitchen and (bottom) checks supplies in the pantry. (Above) John F. Kennedy plays with his children, Caroline and baby John, in the White House nursery as Maud Shaw, their "nanny," looks on.

for all the lights in the mansion. The government, West replied. How much did it cost a month? LBJ wanted to know. About $3,000, West said. The President reached over and with typical flamboyance emphatically turned off the bedroom light.

It was the beginning of his campaign to cut down on the number of lights burning in the White House. He'd prowl the White House himself at night, turning off the lights.

One night a carpenter was working in the White House shop under the North Portico. Suddenly the room was plunged into darkness. The carpenter uttered an oath and demanded to know who had turned off the lights. "I did," said a voice in a familiar Texas accent. It was the President. "I didn't realize you fellows worked so late," Johnson said.

Johnson had another special desire. He wanted his shower to perform exactly as the one in his Washington home, The Elms, did. Engineers were called in, and a new shower was custom-built for the President. Then another, and another and another and another. None satisfactory. A special water tank, with its own pump, was installed in a stairwell closet. Still not satisfactory.

"We kept designing, redesigning, tearing out, installing and fooling with that shower until Lyndon Johnson moved out of the White House," West wrote. "Despite all the talk of saving in electricity, we spent thousands and thousands of dollars, not counting the man-hours, trying to build a shower to please him. It was the strongest, most elaborate shower we'd ever had, with about six different nozzles at different heights, directing spray at every part of the body."

When Richard Nixon became President he looked under the bed that both Kennedy and Johnson had used. He discovered a maze of wires tangled on the floor. They were telephone connections going to dozens of direct lines, remote-control wires for the television sets, and other wires running in different directions.

"Take it all out, whatever it is," President Nixon ordered. "All I need is one line to the operator. She can find anyone else for me."

After he had used the Lyndon Johnson shower, Nixon had another wish. He wanted all the shower heads turned back to normal pressure.

Even the eccentricities or excessive requirements of an occasional presidential guest can be enough to throw the staff into inner turmoil. When Alexander Woollcott, the acerbic critic, was a guest at Franklin Roosevelt's White House, he bedeviled the staff with requests for service around the clock and with demands for his own guests to be shown to his room at all hours. And when King George and Queen Mary of Great Britain came to the White House as the first English sovereigns to visit America, their requirements were enough to make any housekeeper blanch, if not quit.

Consider, for example, the task facing the White House housekeeper for that 1939 state visit. To attend properly to Their Majesties' comfort, the British supplied the White House with the following document:

General Remarks Concerning the Sovereigns and Their Suites

In all rooms: No bolsters—two pillows. Notepaper—penholders, inkstands, writing pads, etc.

Ladies-in-waiting: Hot-water bottle (belonging to them) in each bed. Two or three glasses and spoons.

Countess Spencer: Thermos bottle of ½ liter to be filled every night with hot milk.

Marshal: Big desk table, and second table for papers. In all bathrooms: Glasses, soap.

Numerous vases to be prepared for the flowers offered to the Queen at the receptions.

Special linen room for the Queen, enabling her second maid to press gowns and linen without the attendance of any outsider.

In that room there should be a large supply of white tissue paper and string of various sizes, to be used when repacking.

In the Queen's wardrobes, hangers should not be placed too high, since Her Majesty seldom wears dresses with trains and her dresses should be easily reached.

Light muslin cloths should be provided with which hanging clothes should be covered.

A second linen room for the King's valet and the suite.

All servants' rooms: Glasses, soap, wastebaskets, notepaper.

There should be, in the room of the King's valet, a large solid table for cleaning shoes.

Newspapers: For Their Majesties: *The Times, Daily Telegraph, Le Figaro, Daily Sketch.*

Never should be produced: *Daily Mirror, Sunday Pictorial, News of the World, Daily Express, Daily Mail* (read, however, by part of the suite and the servants).

Breakfast and Refreshments

HIS MAJESTY
8:00 A.M.   Plain tea
9:15 A.M.   Complete breakfast with tea, toast, fruit, bacon, and eggs.

HER MAJESTY
8:00 A.M.   Plain tea
9:15 A.M.   Complete breakfast with tea, toast, and fruit.

Service is always made separately, on trays, the latter prepared by private servants of Their Majesties.

Whenever Their Majesties come home, tea should always be kept ready for them. Moreover, when they come back at midnight, ham sandwiches should be prepared.

The King generally brings his own liquor and spirits. His footman will need a tray with sets of glasses, pump and crushed ice, decanters of lemon and orange juice, and everything necessary for the preparation of cocktails and various drinks.

In all rooms a tray with mineral water in ice, and glasses, should be constantly renewed.

Fruit is not kept in apartments, but is often asked for during the day.

Suggestions for the Furnishing of Her Majesty's Room

Large Bed.
No bolster—two pillows.
Bed cushion supplied by Her Majesty's maid.
Light, but warm, blankets with silk cover.,
No eiderdown coverlet—a soft silk cover folded in four on the foot of the
  bed, with one corner turned up.
Bedside table with lamp.

Dressing Room or Boudoir

Dressing table perfectly lighted day and night, with armchair of corresponding height.
Near the dressing table a small table with drawers for hairdressing and
  toilet articles. This table should be easily removable.
Very comfortable settee with soft wool blanket.
One or two ash trays and matches for the King. The Queen does not
  smoke.
On the desk: Inkstand with blue ink; thin penholder with "J" pen (or
  similar make) of medium size; red pencil; blue pencil; ordinary black
  pencils with very sharp points; ordinary and typewriter erasers.

Suggestions for the Furnishing of His Majesty's Room

Large bed "de Milieu" (in center of panel) with the head against the
  wall. (Never with the side against the wall.)
No bolster—two pillows.
Special bolster supplied by His Majesty's valet.
Warm, but light, blankets with silk cover.
Very soft eiderdown quilt, which can be accordian-pleated at the foot of
  the bed.
On each side of the bed a bedside table with lamp.
In the bathroom or bedroom (according to possibility) and preferably in

window recess on account of light, a dressing table with triple mirror, high enough to enable contemplating oneself when standing.

Very comfortable settee.

Ash trays, matches, cigars, and cigarettes for guests. His Majesty having his own cigarettes.

Great number of hangers; some of them with wide back slightly curved; others with a double bar for trousers; no special clip hangers for trousers.

On desk an inkstand with two inkwells, one full of blue-black the other of red ink.

No toweled bathrobe. His Majesty prefers large bath towels.

To be ready to supply, if requested, garnet-red and white carnations for boutonnieres.

Nearly twenty years later Their Majesties' daughter Queen Elizabeth II was a guest in the White House. The procedure for her was no less elaborate than for her father. As the climax for her visit, the Eisenhowers gave their most elegant state dinner.

"It was quite an operation," J. B. West recalled, "one that required swift, delicate and silent movement. We'd labored over it for days, rehearsing carpenters, butlers and doormen for their part."

As chief usher, a misnomer as a title, West held an indispensable position at the White House. The official U.S. Civil Service Commission position description for that job spells out what seems impossible:

• Subject only to the general direction of the President of the United States, serves as "Chief Usher" of the White House. As such is the general manager of the Executive Mansion, and is delegated full responsibility for directing the administrative, fiscal, and personnel functions involved in the management and operation of the Executive Mansion and grounds, including construction, maintenance, and remodeling of the Executive Mansion.

• Is responsible for the preparation and justification of budget estimates covering administrative and operating expenses, and for the construction and maintenance projects of the Executive Mansion . . . , as well as for the allotment, control, and proper expenditure of funds appropriated for these purposes.

• Is responsible for the direction and supervision of the activities of approximately one hundred employees of the President's household including their selection, appointment, placement, promotion, separation, disciplinary action, etc. In addition, exercises responsibility over the mechanical and maintenance forces in connection with the maintenance and repair of buildings and grounds.

• Serves as the receptionist at the White House, and as such is responsible for receiving and caring for all personal and official guests calling on the President or the First Lady. These guests include, among others, members of the Congress and their families, members of the Judicial Branch, governors, foreign dignitaries, and heads of state. Is responsible for arranging for accommodations for house guests, their comfort, their acquaintance with the customs of the household, etc. Is responsible and arranges for all personal and official entertainments, receptions, dinners, etc., in the Executive Mansion, which frequently include the heads of sovereign states, and several hundred persons. Is responsible for the procurement of all food consumed by the President's family and their guests. Makes personal appointments for the President and other members of his official family.

• Is responsible for answering a large volume of correspondence regarding the Executive Mansion, its history and furnishings, historical subjects, sightseeing, Congressional requests with regard to the Mansion and Grounds, State functions, etc.

• Is completely responsible for the efficient operation, cleanliness, and maintenance of the 123 rooms of the Executive Mansion containing 1,600,000 cubic feet; $2,000,000 of mechanical and air-conditioning equipment.

Under the Nixons and Fords, the chief usher's incredibly difficult job has been filled by Rex Scouten, a veteran White House employee with twenty-five years' service. He is responsible for eighty-six domestic employees who comprise a small, tightly knit group, protective of the President and his family, proud of their own roles, and almost never becoming the subject of notice in the press. They speak for publication rarely, and then only guardedly. They are not the source of White House gossip. They are loyal and hardworking. In fact, many of them regularly work a six-day week. None of them actually lives at the White House: There are no employees in residence there. But there are times when one or two, such as Scouten or the maître d'hôtel, John Ficklin, spend the night if they are working late and have to be in early the next day.

There have always been many White Houses: the public White House as seen through the iron railing around the estate or on the daily tours, the private White House upstairs in the family living quarters, the professional White House emanating from the Oval Office and extending throughout the West Wing and across the driveway into the Executive Office Building, the social White House of the inaugural balls, state dinners, and formal receptions, and the historic White House, wreathed in black in days of national trauma, aglow with lights burning late into the night in times of crisis, and decked with flags and bunting in periods when presidential power is passed normally from hand to hand. All of

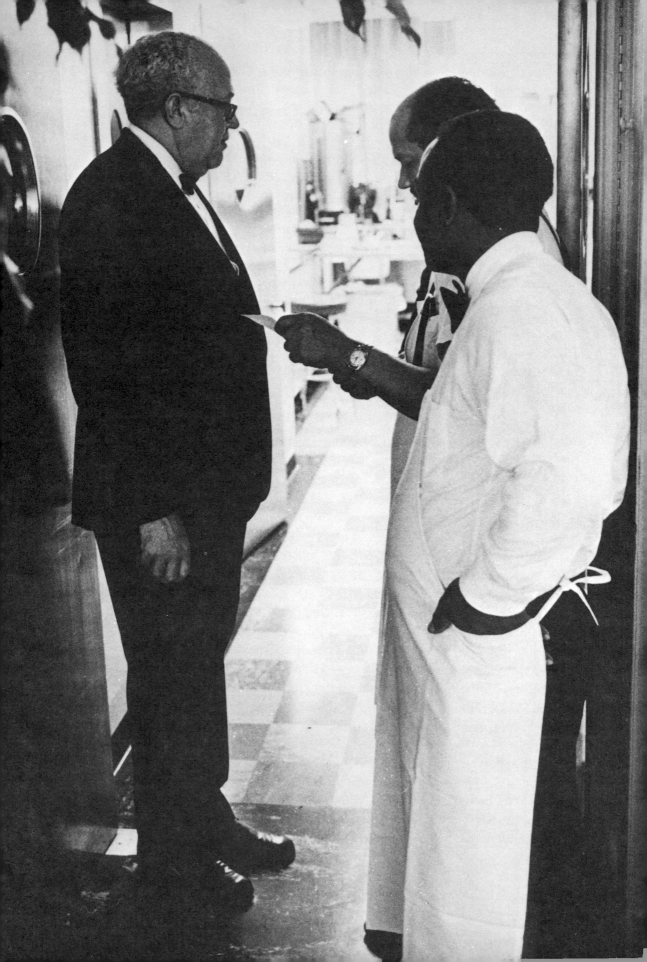

these activities always center around one person, the President of the United States.

For this principal servant of the American people, the years have brought many changes in the roles he must fill and in the magnitude of the problems he faces. For his chief aides—the press secretaries, advisers, speech writers, and counselors who shape each administration—there have also come great changes and new complexities. Many of these people must do their jobs in the full glare of public notice. But, for the behind-the-scenes workers, there has been less in the way of basic change.

These men and women still perform their jobs with the same self-effacing dignity and efficiency as in the past. While great events swirl around them, they continue with the daily, mundane tasks that make it possible for the President and his family to live and work. It might even be said that without them an American President would find it difficult to function at all.

Their White House—the working White House—remains a remarkable example of continuity. It is an enduring link between the American past and present.

54

House and Home Today

From Lafayette Park, with its fountains, plantings, park benches, and heroic statuary, the scene across Pennsylvania Avenue is instantly recognizable. The White House in a photograph taken on a dark and glowering day in 1975 looks scarcely different than it did in the first Mathew Brady photograph of the Executive Mansion, reproduced on page 10. The home of Presidents seems to stand apart, cut off from the traffic and noise of Washington, surrounded by an iron fence, and set off by acres of immaculately landscaped grounds. There is no visible activity.

The picture is misleading. From early morning, when the tourists line up three abreast on the west side of the building, unseen here, to await the hour for the public tours to begin, until late at night, the White House is a center of intense movement. The public sees a fragment of the working White House. They encounter the guards, who check their bags and belongings before permitting them to enter the East Wing and then go on into the mansion. But they see the familiar state rooms—the

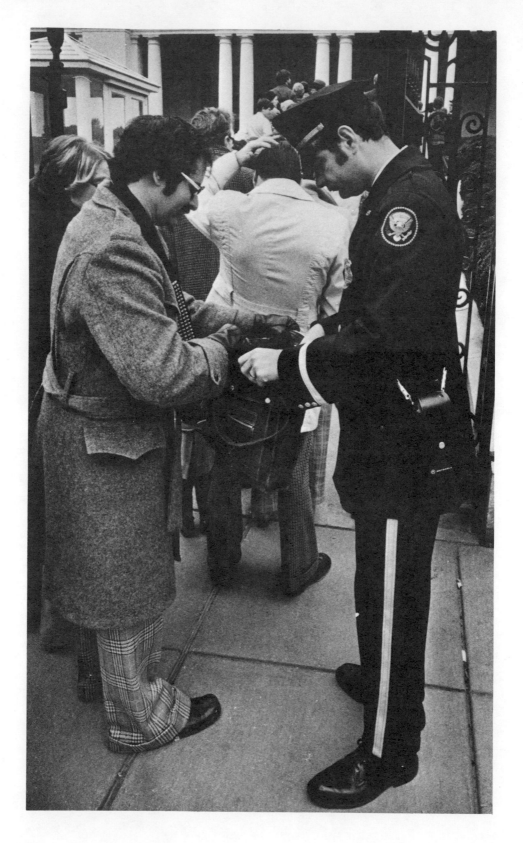

56

East Room, the Green Room, the Blue Room, the State Dining Room, the Cross Hall and entrance hall—all bare of people. They see the antique furniture, the paintings, the draperies, and the carpets and are struck by a sense of history—but they do not see the keepers of this history, who polish and dust and keep these heirlooms of the American people in repair. They catch glimpses of the doorman and perhaps the chief usher or a White House aide. Then they buy their souvenirs and depart, ready to tell one and all they have visited the President's House.

What they never witness are the private and professional sides of the White House at work. Today, as in the past, the basic functions necessary to smooth running of the White House continue day in and day out.

Upstairs, in the family quarters, a maid is changing the bed linens in the Lincoln Room, attending to the small bath, and arranging the table settings where a portrait of Mrs. Lincoln and an old rocker contrast with the pushbutton telephone and extension lines.

IN THIS ROOM
ABRAHAM LINCOLN
SIGNED THE
EMANCIPATION PROCLAMATION
OF JANUARY 1 1863
WHEREBY FOUR MILLION SLAVES
WERE GIVEN THEIR FREEDOM
AND SLAVERY FOREVER PROHIBITED
IN THESE UNITED STATES

Upstairs at the White House, every room is cleaned and dusted every day, including guest rooms not in use. "We never know when they will be used," said a White House employee. "We have to be ready on an instant's notice for a guest." Some hand laundry and pressing are also done upstairs, but the bulk of the laundry is handled by two people. They work in the commercial-sized White House laundry.

As the tourists are completing their visit at noon, upstairs in the dining room the President and his family are being served lunch while a wood fire crackles in the fireplace.

Serving the President is not the only task for those who work at the White House. They also serve the President's family. Outside, in the White House driveway, Steve Ford, the President's son, is working on his motorcycle. But not alone. That cannot happen if you're the President's son or daughter. Steve is being watched closely by a White House policeman and a Secret Service agent.

If the President and his daughter, Susan, want to get away for a moment's relaxation with their dog on the lawn, police keep attentive watch on them from a discreet distance.

And always in the background at the White House are the ubiquitous workmen performing their daily—and endless—maintenance tasks. One man works full-time to wash all the windows. "We'll never find another person like that again," one White House employee remarked. "He's got his job down to a science." When he finishes with the windows, he then washes and polishes all the chandeliers. Other White House aides pay no attention as he stands on a ladder in the vaulted-arch hallway on the ground floor, out of sight of the public tours.

In the President's Oval Office another workman waxes and buffs the floors. He already has finished vacuuming the carpet. Immediately after the tourists leave, other employees go to work waxing and polishing all the floors in the public part of the mansion. "You get used to seeing the floors in such beautiful spick-and-span condition that I'm always startled when I come through about noon and see the difference in just two hours," one White House aide said. "It really needs cleaning after that." The antique furniture is also polished daily. With lemon oil, never wax.

The carpets are often vacuumed as many as six times a day because of the numerous functions held there. The marble entrances and floor of the North Lobby are also mopped that often. Brass is polished throughout, including the brass on the exterior of each of the twenty-eight fireplaces.

Grand as the White House seems to the public on the cursory daily tours, the actual building does not convey an impression of vast splendor. Sedate, charming, beautifully furnished and built for ages to come, it also seems today too small for the tasks required of it. Already the storage space is lacking. Firewood, for instance, is now stored in the old tunnel built as a bomb shelter during World War II. Because of insufficient space, only enough wood for immediate needs is kept. There is only one fair-sized storage room for furniture. Other furniture is stacked in different rooms.

One small service elevator often is taxed far beyond its originally planned capacity. In it furniture for various functions has to be carried back and forth.

"We went through a period recently when the President was having breakfasts at 7:30 and dinners that same night," said one aide who worked in the Ford White House. "It's extremely difficult. It required different equipment, so we had to change for each function. It's a tremendous amount of work."

And the staff, large as it seems, is called upon to do much more than in the past. As one White House employee put it: "We have a very small staff and they work a tremendous amount of overtime. That's the only way we can meet our requirements. We're not overstaffed by any means. The only way we can operate is to have a small staff where everyone knows a little bit about everybody else's job. If something comes up at four o'clock today then whoever's here at least can help the others do what has to be done. It's a team effort, and the team has to stick together."

As in any home in the 1970s, the cost of running the White House keeps increasing. For 1975, the White House requested Congress to appropriate $1,744,000 to provide basic maintenance, repair, heating, and lighting. Given their responsibilities, the eighty-six employees who make up the domestic staff are certainly not overpaid. Their average annual salary comes to $12,415 a year.

A stroll through the White House basement, which the public is not permitted to see, shows another side of White House work that belies the common impression of a palatial establishment.

The kitchen staff is small—five cooks, plus a pastry chef. Each day one person purchases all the food for the White House, following through on orders placed the day before. Where the White House obtains its food, how it is transported to the kitchen, and what steps are taken to ensure that it is safe are all official White House secrets. It is well known that for many years standard procedure has required that all gifts of food for the President be taken under Secret Service guard to food- and drug-inspection laboratories for analysis.

All the food is placed in a storeroom off the kitchen, and then is meticulously checked off to account for where it goes. Food for the White House staff mess is paid for out of the annual congressional appropriation, for the President and his family out of their pockets, for state dinners out of State Department funds, for a political function by the political party's national committee, for certain other functions by various government agencies involved. The bookkeeping involved for this purchasing-and-dispensing operation alone is enormous.

Around the corridor from these rooms, and near the kitchen, are two other rooms where daily work proceeds with precision. In the flower shop fresh flowers are brought in each day from commercial establishments in Washington. They are arranged in bouquets and then placed throughout the Executive Mansion. For formal social events, special floral arrangements are made there.

Six carpenters work next door in the carpenters' shop; they are charged with handling all construction in the house and are always busy at major jobs or smaller tasks like repairing chairs. They take care of the ordinary furniture; when the more valuable antiques need repair, the White House sends them out to specialists.

Hidden away inside the White House are many other activities the public never is permitted to see. One of the endless jobs that grows in complexity year by year involves the White House mail. In the early years of the White House, when the postal service was still in its formative stages, relatively little mail was delivered. But with the coming of the railroads the President's mail began to multiply. President Millard Fillmore, in a public address, commented on what seemed to him the stupendous amount of mail he was receiving. It was then averaging more than one hundred letters a day.

Theodore Roosevelt's ascension to the presidency created a dramatic increase in the volume. The popular Teddy began getting as many as fifteen hundred letters a day. So vast was their outpouring that a special department was created at the Washington post office just to handle the White House letters, periodicals, and packages.

Ira R. T. Smith (page 29, bottom right) chief of White House mails under nine Presidents beginning with McKinley, described the torrent of mail in the early days of the first Roosevelt administration as being "like an avalanche."

"Everything was turned upside down," he said, "the mail poured in. We began taking on clerks. Before long we had fifty people handling mail. After the first week we were 450,000 letters behind—almost half a million letters that hadn't been touched. We had mail up and down the corridors and even over in the State Department. It took us six months to catch up."

Smith's mail problems in those early years were nothing compared to the present. By the Truman Administration bagloads of mail were delivered three times a day by truck to the White House. The White House mail room then had to handle two to three times the volume in Theodore Roosevelt's day. And after a major presidential speech or message the volume soared to as high as 50,000 pieces of mail. During President Kennedy's first two weeks 87,000 letters were delivered to the White House mail room.

For years Ira Smith himself was in charge of seeing that nothing dangerous was mailed to the White House. His methods now seem quaint, particularly when viewed from an era of sophisticated explosive devices and letter bombs.

"I listened for ticking," Smith explained, "opened packages at the end of a pole and dunked others in oil. Did it for years—and never lost a President."

By the post–World War II period the processing of the mail and the methods employed to protect the President and White House occupants were radically different. First, all the mail was fluoroscoped. If anything of a suspicious nature turned up, it was immediately x-rayed. The Secret Service was called instantly if anything of a possibly lethal nature was detected. The agents were trained in the handling and disposal of explosives.

Now the security around the White House mail is so tight that a photographer is not permitted to see or take a picture of the process by which the mail is examined.

On an average day in the Ford White House some five thousand letters are delivered. The mail now comes in twice each morning, and again in the afternoon if necessary. After security checks are made, the letters are opened and read by a team of fifteen analysts. They sort the mail and mark it according to content. Requests for autographed photographs of the President go in one pile, comments gauging public opinion on the issues of the day in others.

By far the largest part of the mail comes from ordinary American citizens who want to express their personal opinions to their President— on such public issues as abortion, aid to Israel, the energy crisis, and the state of the economy.

Once the letters are categorized they are then sorted for distribution to appropriate offices in the White House, as well as to specific federal agencies for their attention and resolution. Letters that would be of particular interest to the President or Mrs. Ford are routed to them.

This flood of mail goes on day after day, year after year. It keeps increasing with the growth of the American population and the ever greater complexity of volatile national issues. In times of crisis or great national debate the amount of mail reaches gigantic proportions. When Gerald Ford pardoned Richard Nixon, for instance, the action prompted 280,000 people to write the President, care of the White House.

The mail room does more than process the incoming letters and packages. It also oversees outgoing mail from the White House. By 1975,

the mail room was supervising the dispatch of some twenty-five hundred such letters each day.

Maintenance of the White House extends beyond the physical walls of the building itself. Throughout the year, groundskeepers supplied by the U.S. Park Service are kept busy tending the shrubs, trees, and flowers that have been planted in every administration from John Adams's to the present.

On the White House grounds today are American elms from John and Abigail Adams, magnolias from Andrew Jackson, scarlet oaks from Benjamin Harrison, Japanese maples from Grover Cleveland, pin oaks from William McKinley, European white birches from Calvin Coolidge, white oaks from Herbert Hoover, little-leaf lindens from Franklin Roosevelt, American boxwood from Harry Truman, black walnut from Dwight Eisenhower, apple trees from John Kennedy, darlington oaks from Lyndon Johnson, giant sequoias from Richard Nixon.

From his Oval Office, Gerald Ford can look out on a gardener digging outside his window or see others pruning branches in the Rose Garden.

As in any home, there are periods in the White House year when snow

must be removed, Christmas trees brought in, wreaths hung, and the exterior decorated for the holiday season. There is one difference, though. The White House is not any home. It must always be the one place where Americans turn for guidance and inspiration from their nation's leader, and nothing that is done to make this house work can interfere either with that symbolic role or with the serious business of governance.

For the Office of the President

There is something mystical about the way the crowds gather around the iron fence surrounding the White House in times of crisis. They appear mysteriously. Silent, grave, they grow in number by the minute until they are massed at the gates staring straight ahead toward the building. They come as witnesses to history, and as citizens wanting to be reassured that the most visible symbol of national purpose still functions and still offers leadership. They gathered that way on the Sunday in December after the Japanese attacked Pearl Harbor, on the soft April day when Franklin Roosevelt died, on the brilliant fall afternoon when John Kennedy was assassinated. And they were there again on the summer day when Richard Nixon became the first President to resign his office. As always, they were solemn and patient, more preoccupied by feelings of sorrow and sadness for a crisis facing their nation than with their personal doubts and fears.

Two of those who gathered at the gate on the day Nixon left office

expressed thoughts that summed up the feelings of many Americans about their White House and their country.

"Think of it," said a tourist from Wheaton, Illinois. "The most beautiful building in the country, right across the street, and the man that lives there, that has worked all his life to get there, has to give it up."

And another visitor from Myrtle Beach, South Carolina, who was looking toward the White House: "Our country will survive. In a way, this is like the Kennedy assassination. It is a sad time for everyone, but we'll pull through."

What they have seen in all these periods of national anguish is the White House standing strong and secure, continuing to work as it always has, carrying out the business of the President and the nation without hesitation. What the public senses, but does not see, is the tension inside the calm exterior of the White House.

On the night Nixon resigned, for instance, while the crowds kept increasing until they filled Lafayette Park across Pennsylvania Avenue, inside the White House people were watching, too. Police and aides and staff workers for the President stood at the office windows, themselves staring out across the lawn toward the iron fence and the park beyond. They also were swept by the history of the moment; some showed their loyalties clearly. One office chair bore the words "Support the President."

SUPPORT THE PRESIDENT

The slogan was intended as support for a particular President, but in fact the White House always supports the President no matter who he may be or what his politics are. Whatever personal loyalties have been built up during one administration must be put aside swiftly, even ruthlessly, for the next occupant of the presidential office. And the work must proceed.

A moment of ceremony, observed by millions across the world, is something more than a fleeting glimpse of an outgoing and an incoming

President walking down a red carpet spread on the White House lawn
before they take their farewells. It is just as much an illustration of how
well the White House works in a period of extreme national stress. The
ceremonial functions move forward smoothly. The carpet is laid. The
helicopter is waiting to carry off the President. The band strikes up the
last salute. The schedule proceeds like clockwork. Then the copter lifts
off. It is scarcely a few feet from the ground when military aides immediately begin rolling up the carpet and removing it from view. They

have begun their work for the new President. They have helped make it possible for him to face the burdens and agonies of decisions in his Oval Office, where the lights often burn until late in the night and the pressures of the job are overwhelming. At times a view from outside its window into the Oval Office shows a President wearily struggling with a problem, wrestling with a thought, and rubbing his forehead with his eyes closed.

In addition to the domestic staff, which has its own role to play in maintaining the home and in serving the President, a small army of professional people works at the White House to ease the President's burdens. Those who work in the West Wing, either on the President's personal staff or in his Executive Office, form the nerve center of the White House. The counselors and advisers and speech writers, the communications specialists, the military aides, the secretaries, and the White House policemen and Secret Service agents—all contribute critical skills toward making it possible for the President to govern.

For all of them, serving the President professionally is their one concern. Theirs are demanding jobs, full of pressures and tensions. The hours are long, the attention to detail exacting, the cumulative strain immense. Yet, strangely, a visitor to the White House does not come away with this sense of terrible pressure. The White House has been operating for so long, in so many times of crisis and challenge, that the working side of the West Wing conveys an atmosphere of calm and unhurried deliberation. At the same time one cannot help being struck with the remarkable efficiency and volume of work accomplished there. It seems effortless. Of course it is not.

The public is most familiar with the scenes of the President himself at work—in his Oval Office, meeting either with advisers clustered around his desk or, for more celebrated company, alone with his Secretary of State; in his cabinet room, surrounded by senior officials of the government; in the ceremonial East Room, chairing a conference on the economy. Many of these daily offerings of the President at work seem antiseptic: Everything looks so neat, so well ordered, that it seems as if little work really is being accomplished—or that the work is being done by the pulling of invisible strings.

A more realistic portrait, one rarely seen but nonetheless one that any executive instantly would recognize, is of the President too busy to take a lunch break, being served at his desk in his office. More unusual but more truthful is the sight of the President's desk covered with work papers with an open looseleaf folder at the side.

Operating out of public view are the offices that are grouped around the President's own in the West Wing, offices where the executive business goes on constantly. The President sometimes has to eat lunch at his

desk; his Press Secretary has to eat meals at his desk each day, beginning with breakfast. The daily schedule of Ron Nessen, Press Secretary under President Ford, tells a lot about the daily demands of the working White House.

His regular day begins at 7 A.M. when a White House limousine picks him up at his home. While driving to the White House, he begins reading two morning papers and a daily news digest prepared for the President. He gets to his office, has breakfast, and studies four other morning

papers taken by the White House. From 8:00 to 8:30 he attends a meeting of key presidential staff aides to discuss upcoming business, intelligence reports, and problems facing the President and the nation. Then he conducts a staff meeting for his own press aides. Next is a meeting with the President, usually alone. It is the first of about three such meetings with the President daily. At 11 A.M. and again about 4 P.M., he conducts a press briefing for the regular correspondents assigned to cover the White House, and must be ready to deal with queries from outside news personnel throughout the day and night.

The Press Secretary's is a long—and exhausting—schedule, but no more so than those of other key West Wing aides to the President. They are on 24-hour call, and must be ready at a moment's notice to leave the White House with the President or assist him in any tasks required.

In other offices throughout the West Wing a visitor finds constant activity, but always carried out in unruffled, unharried style. Secretaries are on their phones, answering questions, arranging details, and preparing to distribute volumes of bulky materials that bear the presidential seal. In this case, it is an economic report of the President, one that will create instant repercussions around the world. In other cases, it will be speeches or transcripts or formal State of the Union messages to Congress to be distributed. All immediately become objects of intense public scrutiny and debate. Other aides are occupied with other tasks: studying photographs, preparing documents and speeches, meeting with experts on the critical issues of the day.

Life in the West Wing is not without its lighter moments. In the Ford White House, the President's dog, Liberty, given free reign of the executive offices, often has been seen indulging in an affectionate moment with busy presidential aides. And the President has been seen snapping his personal photographer.

The President's business office extends from his Oval Office, throughout the West Wing, and over into the next door Executive Office Building, where he also has his own office and is served by people who work for him. The Executive Office Building, formerly the State, War, and Navy Departments, is actually an extension of the White House, and some vital Executive Mansion business is conducted there.

Behind a locked door in the basement of the EOB—as the Executive Office Building is known to all who work there—carefully guarded by a series of White House police checks, is one of the indispensable parts of modern presidential government. That is where the main White House switchboard is located. The operators who work in that fifteen- by twenty-foot room, facing the tangle of wires and plugs on the board in front of them, are the conduit for instant communications around the world. As an operator works, her hand moving so fast it becomes a blur even to the camera, she keeps a pad ready to jot down messages and numbers. As the day goes on, her pile of memo notes grows at her right side.

The switchboard itself is remarkable for what it says about the intricate web of communications woven about the President. There are plugs to reach the President on his elevator, in his oval sitting room, in the movie room. Each goes only to the President: "Elev Pres" is carefully distinguished from "Elev WH" for instance. Marked on the board are lines to Key Biscayne and San Clemente that not only evoke an era from the immediate presidential past but also indicate the complex routing of calls that pass through the White House switchboard from points around the globe. The switchboard clearly demonstrates how dependent the President and the working White House are on telephonic, to say nothing of cable and coded, communications. The phones in the White House are always lighted, extension lines flashing on, offering clues to the volume of business conducted out of the West Wing.

Many jobs that are done almost without notice are part of the standard routine of serving the President. If, for instance, he has a speech to deliver in Washington (or anywhere else, for that matter), one aide sees to it that the presidential seal is posted on the podium seconds before he begins his address. The aide approaches, centers the seal, and affixes it to the podium—right side up. As he leaves, the President opens his folder containing his text and begins his address.

This little-noticed function takes place with split-second timing, as do most of the tasks performed for the President. At the White House, the presidential appointments secretary lives in a world dictated by time. He checks his watch constantly and goes over the schedule for the next presidential appointment.

Neither public nor press normally observes these inner workings of the presidential office. In the West Wing press lobby, built during the Nixon Administration over the pool in which Roosevelt, Truman, Eisenhower, Kennedy, and Johnson swam, once the daily news briefings are held there is often time for a game of chess before the President conducts a press

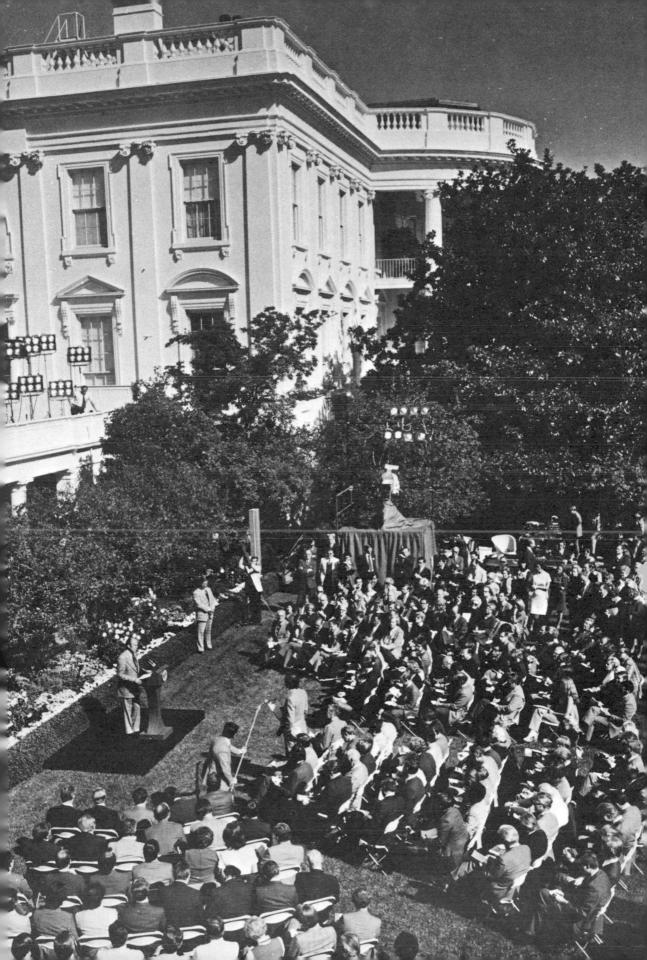

conference. Depending on the weather and the President's wishes, these televised full-dress press conferences can be held outside in the Rose Garden or, in the scene most familiar to Americans, in the formality of the East Room.

But once a conference is completed there is no time for leisure. Television correspondents immediately take up positions on the grounds out-

side the West Wing to offer reportage and commentary on the news the President has just made. While these reports are being given, work continues inside the West Wing.

The White House proper has been standing at 1600 Pennsylvania Avenue N.W., in the federal city of Washington, for one hundred seventy-five years. But in fact the White House as home, office, and symbol operates around the world. Whenever a President leaves the Executive Mansion, if only to go to church, many of those who work for him inside the White House travel with him. He is attended by aides, press personnel, his personal physician, drivers who operate the fleet of specially equipped limousines out of the White House garage—and always, everywhere, Secret Service agents.

Protecting the President has become so visible and critical a part of modern White House operations that most people assume the Secret Service net has always been as tight as it is now. Actually, it is only since World War II that protecting the President has become so massive a job.

Even during Franklin Roosevelt's first two administrations in the 1930s an air of informality prevailed around the White House. Anybody could walk right through the gates and up to the White House without being stopped. Police were not installed at the gates until the coming of World War II. Before that, a number of recorded incidents revealed how easy it was to penetrate the protection thrown around the President.

Once, when Theodore Roosevelt was President, a taxi drove up to the front door of the mansion and a man in full evening dress, cloak, and high hat stepped out. He said he had an appointment with the President. The policeman on duty at the door immediately ushered him inside, and he was taken into the Red Room. Roosevelt talked to him, and then quietly rang a bell summoning the chief usher. "Take this crank out of here," he said. When the man was searched, a high-caliber gun was found in his rear pocket.

During Herbert Hoover's administration a strange man walked into the White House dining room, where he was promptly seated with eight or ten guests. Then the man got up, approached the President, and said, "I want to see you." Secret Service agents were called, but not before the man could have attacked the President. He turned out to be harmless.

Such incidents could not occur today. Not only is it increasingly difficult to get into the White House (even those with White House passes must turn over their briefcases, tape recorders, and typewriters to be inspected by police at the gates), but when a President travels he is always surrounded by agents.

A limousine, dubbed the "gun car," which carries agents and the

President's personal White House physician, always follows the President's car. The moment the motorcade stops, the agents jump from the running boards and race forward to surround the President and First Family.

When the President and his wife return to their limousine, which bears the presidential seal, they are surrounded by watchful agents. On the street, other agents keep a wary eye on the scene around them, even employing their limousine rear mirrors. Then the motorcade leaves with agents running to catch up as the limousines drive off for the return to the White House.

All the agents are armed, but seldom are their weapons openly displayed. At Grand Junction, Colorado, after a presidential airport arrival, an agent watches intently, a submachine gun ready for action. The names

of most agents are not known to the public, but during the Ford Administration one man became the subject of articles. He is Richard E. Keiser, the Secret Service agent in charge of the White House detail. Keiser, who always accompanies the President, and often stands next to him, look so much like Gerald Ford that he might be his double. In fact, he has been called "Mr. President" by people who think he is Mr. Ford.

A President cannot do anything in public without his phalanx of agents. They are there if he shakes hands through a fence with citizens at an airport or at a political rally, if he takes a break and plays golf, or if he rides through the loneliness of the American desert. When his plane, Air Force One, is ready to depart the motorcade forms another protective cordon.

110

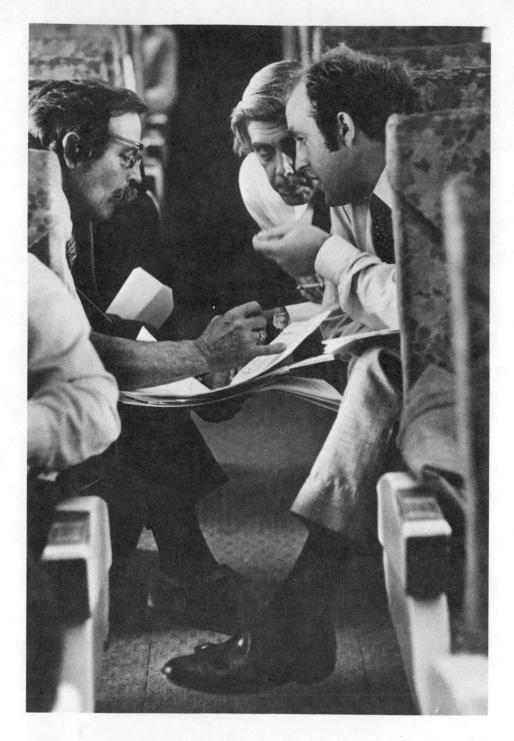

But the agents are not the only White House workers who travel with, and offer support to, the President. His advance men, who prepare the way for the next presidential stop, huddle in midair over last-minute details. And whenever a President travels there is always another immense

job that must be accomplished flawlessly—the moving of the baggage and special equipment that accompany the Chief Executive.

Anyone who has ever traveled with a President comes away impressed by the White House Transportation Office. It is responsible for not only White House equipment and presidential luggage but often piles of baggage for as many as two hundred working press personnel. The early-

morning scenes of a room filled with luggage, and of Transportation Office personnel charged with moving it to the next presidential stop, are familiar on all White House trips. Not as familiar is the sight of a transportation aide, wired for action, as he hooks up a two-way radio that permits him to keep in constant contact with all White House movement; nor of the communications aides who monitor and record for the archives all presidential remarks during a lunch break, while all the time themselves staying in electronic contact through ear plugs.

When a President travels, the working White House goes with him: aboard Air Force One, where he is interviewed by reporters in flight, and where he remains in constant communication with key advisers (and where his staff finds that lunch aboard the plane must be taken on the

run, and between phone calls and presidential documents). While the President's plane leads the way, behind him another government aircraft carries the main press party It, too, is a place for work. Presidential aides are kept busy, often to the point of appearing harried, as they proceed up and down the aisles distributing advance speech texts, transcripts of presidential remarks from the last stop prepared by the White House, and itineraries and official briefing material.

Before the President's plane lands, other White House personnel already have attended to a number of important jobs. One of the most sensitive is seeing that the President's special phone, which permits him to be in contact for any moment of crisis through the White House switchboard, has been set up on the landing strip. As soon as the President departs, the phone is taken away to the next area.

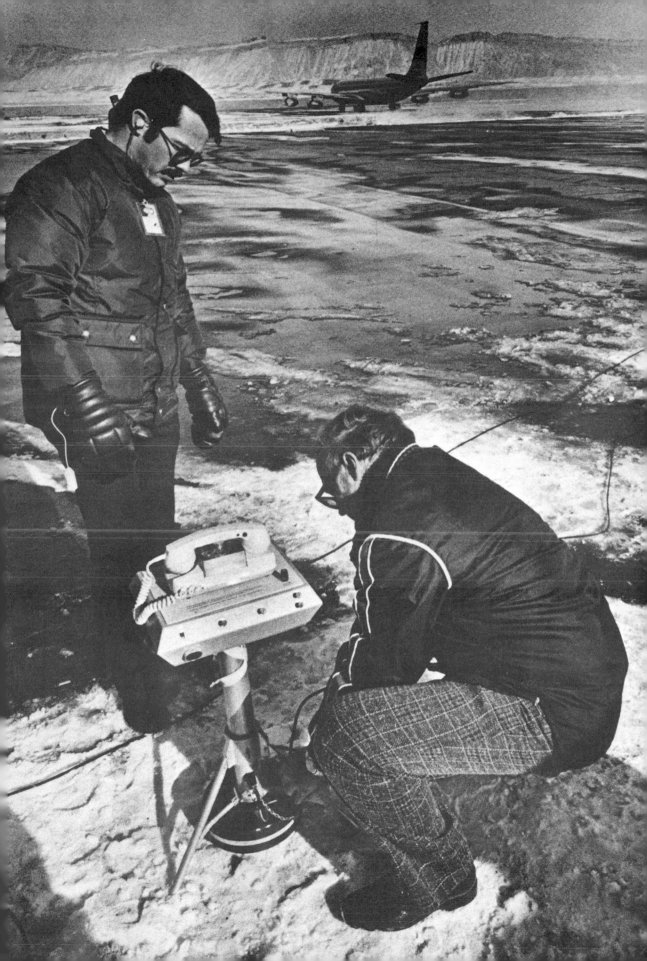

These presidential trips, which may carry the Chief Executive around the world, are demanding and exhausting. The wonder is that so many vital jobs are handled so smoothly. But they must be; nothing involving the President of the United States in his White House on the wing can be left to chance.

There are times when every occupant of the White House needs a moment of relaxation and a chance to escape from the constant glare of public scrutiny. In earlier and more innocent presidential eras, the First Families customarily left the White House each summer for a working vacation. Thus the term "the summer White House." The summer White House, of course, was wherever the President happened to stay.

In more recent years, Presidents have used a closer refuge for their moments away from desk and mansion. What Franklin Roosevelt called "Shangri-La," during his frequent departures from Washington during World War II, is a presidential retreat in the nearby Catoctin Mountains

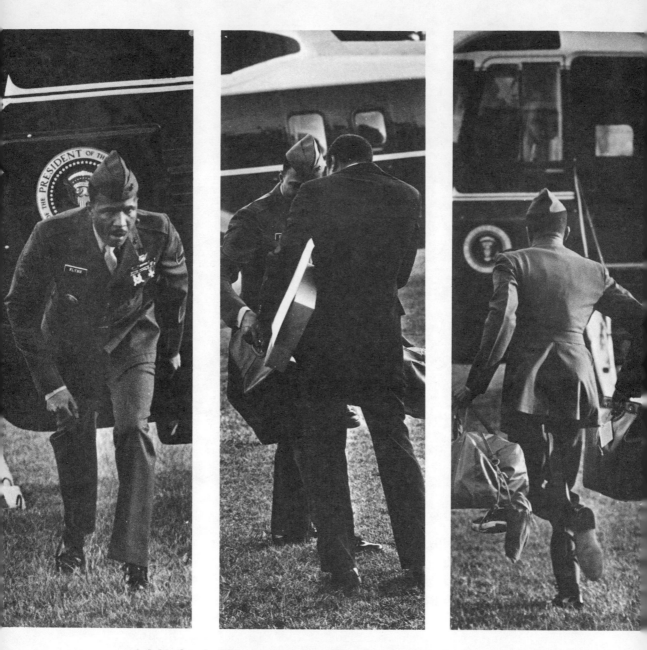

of Maryland. There, in what Dwight D. Eisenhower renamed Camp David, as it is still called, the President can get away easily for either a weekend or an evening.

A helicopter bearing the presidential seal stands ready at his command to carry him away from the White House to Camp David. The copter lands on the South Lawn, and a military aide races from it toward the mansion. He is met by a White House butler who hands over the personal luggage for the President and his family. Then the aide races back to the copter, and the journey begins.

The change from the formality of life in the Washington White House is sudden. Behind fences patrolled by military guards and watched by Secret Service agents, members of the presidential family are given an opportunity to dress casually, stroll on the extensive lawns (and nurse a baby deer, if they wish), and share moments of much needed privacy.

The President never entirely escapes from the demands of his job. Even in the informal setting of Camp David, accompanied by aides and military personnel, work continues. A typical sight is that of the President's military aide sitting on the back of a sofa in the President's camp conferring by phone on official business.

If President Ford wishes to take a break with his daughter, Susan, and ride a snowmobile both he and she are constantly watched by a Secret agent. If he goes for a swim in mid-February in the heated Camp David pool (joined by Liberty), the moment he steps from the pool he is attended by an aide.

But though spring weekend or a winter's outing in the snow offers the President and his family a necessary respite from some of their responsibilities, the White House always beckons them back to affairs of state. From the informality of their Catoctin retreat, they must return to their official roles. Often, they appear in the most formal of ceremonial settings.

Social Symbol

In the United States, where royalty cannot command and a court does not exist, only one invitation serves as a summons that must be obeyed. The envelopes, small, stiff, and white, are mailed to the mighty of the land—the executives, the artists, the entertainers, the leaders of Congress, and the judiciary. In elegant script painstakingly crafted by White House calligraphers under the embossed seal of the President of the United States, the invitation bears the simple and time-honored phrase "The President and Mrs. Ford request the pleasure of the company of . . ." Another small card, in the same fine calligrapher's hand, explains the purpose of the evening: "On the occasion of the visit of His Royal Highness, the King of . . ."

The occasion, of course, is a state dinner given by the President on behalf of a distinguished foreign guest. As Donnie Radcliffe of the *Washington Post* has written:

To have dinner at the White House is to climb a top rung of the political

129

ladder. It is an event that is as close as any this nation has to a command performance and one where the lines of protocol are both numerous and intricately woven. . . . In all administrations, such dinners serve manifold functions. By definition, they are tools of international relations. But they also allow the President—through the invitation list—to pay political debts, lobby for congressional votes, recognize campaign contributors, honor various segments of society from science, labor and business to sports and the arts. And they also serve as a means—particularly for the Ford administration—to heal wounds, invite back those political forces who were left out in the cold and, perhaps, neutralize old animosities.

To the public, a state dinner is the one national event that transcends political party or personality, economic class or social status. It symbolizes the most elegant aspect of American life. It is also an occasion in which all the disparate functions of the White House come together in tightly controlled, smoothly functioning fashion. Social aides and security personnel, maids and butlers, cooks and military escorts, carpenters and electricians, calligraphers and press staff, musicians and color guards—all have their specific parts to play, upstairs and downstairs and throughout the Executive Mansion. The White House wears its most attractive dress on these occasions. Rooms where tourists have flocked are thrown open to the select invited guests. Entertainment and elaborate dinners and cocktails and dancing proceed with clockwork precision, yet without a sense of haste or too heavy a regimented schedule. It seems so effortlessly arranged that few of those present are aware of all the intense planning and effort that go into only one evening at the White House.

The largest formal function during Richard Nixon's years in office is a case in point.

A dinner was planned to salute the American prisoners of war who had returned from North Vietnamese confinement. Although the event was held outdoors to accommodate 1,326 persons, it was served as a state dinner. The White House staff planned for that one occasion for two months. A vast tent had to be built outside, with a stage constructed within it. Nearby were dressing-room tents for entertainers and military field kitchens to assist with the cooking. To set and serve that number in formal state-dinner style required an extraordinary effort. Each round table was set with ten chairs, a tablecloth, china, various pieces of silver, wine glasses, a menu, nut dishes, matches bearing the words "The President's House," and a centerpiece. In all, approximately thirty-nine thousand separate pieces were used by those guests on that one evening at the White House.

That it works at all is a marvel. That it works so well seems a miracle.

Planning for a state dinner often begins months in advance between the emissaries of the two governments, but the final stage of completing the arrangements begins several weeks before the actual event. Each state dinner has its own theme, tailored to the evening and the guest of honor.

Betty Ford, the President's wife, in an interview with Donnie Radcliffe explained her philosophy in attempting to set exactly the right tone. "I'm trying to promote American art in all forms," she said. "We've had Steuben glass, silver museum pieces, and at the dinner for England's Prime Minister Wilson, historic old decoys because we knew he's an amateur ornithologist. We wouldn't have done it if we knew he hated birds."

She personally takes a hand in how the guests are seated.

"We don't put all political, or all art, or all anything at any one table," she explained. "We try for a mixture—a cabinet officer, someone from the visiting country, a movie star."

Long before the guests begin arriving shortly before eight o'clock, the White House has been busily at work preparing for the evening. Early in the morning the chief usher and the maître d'hôtel confer about the menu and the food preparation. Round tables are carried into the State

Dining Room, and places for ten are set. One complete table is set first
by the butlers and waiters as a model for all the others; tablecloths, china,
silver, red- and white-wine glasses, champagne glasses, nut dishes, linen

napkins, the centerpiece, the dinner menu, and a card bearing the guest's name, graced by the same fine art of the White House calligraphers.

These dinners normally are held for 100 guests. On each occasion there are 800 pieces of table china, 800 items of gold or silver flatware, and 400 crystal goblets with stems to be set, served, and unobtrusively removed. (All of this service is washed by hand.)

Maids fill silver holders with ten brands of cigarettes and place them, with ash trays, on each table. One woman sets and lights all the candles.

While these tasks are being performed, other work proceeds throughout the day. A platform to be set up for the entertainment in the East Room is wheeled through the front entrance of the White House. A harp is

carried into the Diplomatic Reception Room, where it will provide background music for the guests during the early reception period. At the North Portico, the formal ceremonial entrance to the White House, two men begin to run a red carpet into the main door. There, the President will officially greet his honored guest.

The logistical details are intricate: where to place the stanchions for photographic coverage, how to arrange with the electricians for the special lighting required, what are the needs of the television networks with their video cameras and cables, and how to coordinate effectively with all the varied White House offices, press and social, as well as the Secret Service and White House police.

In the kitchen, the normally small staff of five, plus a pastry chef, has been expanded. Three more women are brought in from outside to assist with the preparations. All have been carefully cleared by the Secret Service, naturally. As the chefs work, the large silver bowls stand by, gleaming, ready to receive the consommé with brandy. The chefs work without stress and strain. This is their calling, the moment of their finest testing—and achievement.

Everywhere, constant coordination and checking take place. A butler runs over a list with the kitchen employees. A dishwasher—believe it or not, the one official White House dishwasher—keeps busy scrubbing by hand the large pots and pans as the chefs finish their work.

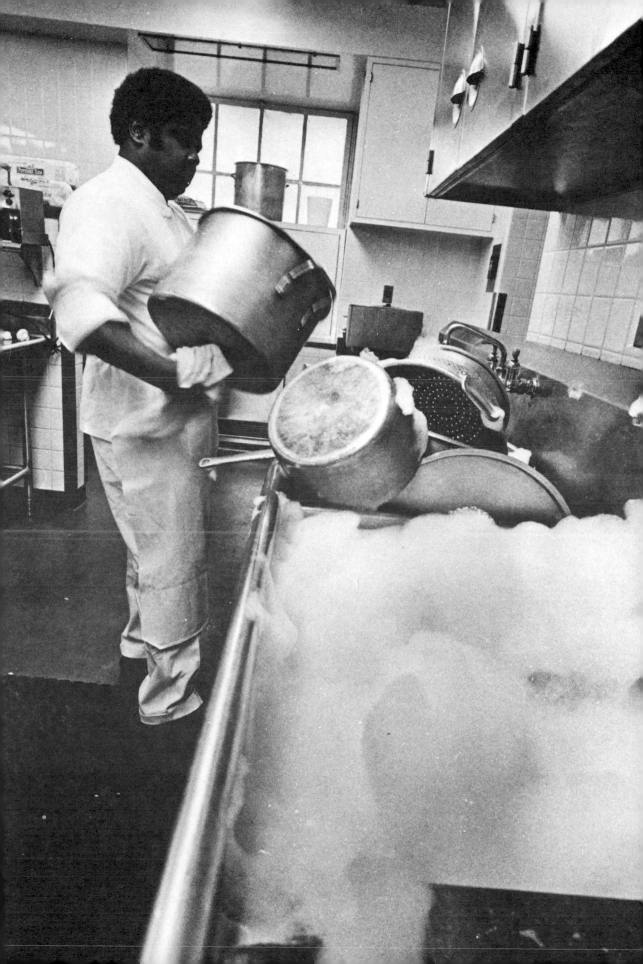

Upstairs, in the family quarters, last-minute preparations are also being made. A military aide, dressed in his most splendid uniform, mans a phone to follow the progress of the distinguished visitor. The foreign leader is now en route by motorcade to the White House. The phone rings again.

The leader is now expected to arrive within two minutes. The President is informed and himself goes over the last-second protocol arrangements before leaving to greet his guest at the main entrance, and then to escort him back upstairs to the family quarters. There, a small reception will be held in the Queen's Room.

The Vice-President's wife is on hand and chats with the First Lady before other guests arrive.

The First Lady also gets specific instructions from a military aide who runs through the exact procedure she will follow as the color guard escorts them back downstairs for the formal reception line. She checks where she will stand, how the honor guard will move, and when.

In the downstairs Library, the contingent of twenty-five social aides, six of them women, quickly checks through the guest list. They are assigned to different doors and rooms. They will escort the guests, and also form an honor guard in the Cross Hall when the President and his visitor make their entrance. For the butlers there is time for one brief break before the arduous evening work begins. They sit in an unused room, waiting. Elsewhere, a workman checks one of the many fires laid earlier.

By now the invited guests are arriving. They come in through the South Portico entrance, carrying their prized invitations. As they enter the Diplomatic Reception Room, they turn over an admittance card sent several days earlier by the White House social office. Their cards are scanned beneath ultraviolet for signs of possible forgery; then, their coats are taken by military aides, and they are ushered into the White House.

The fires are blazing and the strains of a harp are heard as they move by the China and Vermeil rooms and the Library and on upstairs through the North Entrance Hall.

At the top of the stairs, standing behind a small table, is Preston Bruce. He is the White House doorman. In his twenty years of service in the President's House he has greeted more dinner guests there than any of the thirty-six men who have been President of the United States. As a guest comes forward he checks the name and hands over a small white envelope containing the number of the table at which the guest will dine.

As Bruce passes out the envelopes, he turns over name cards to a White House social aide. Like everything else connected with the White House, this aide demonstrates that nothing has been left to chance. His job is to announce the guests as they walk into the East Room; his voice has been judged to set exactly the right tone by the White House social secretary.

Once the guests enter the East Room to await the President and go through the receiving room, they are offered mixed drinks on silver trays. If they smoke, butlers light their cigarettes or cigars.

By now the President has greeted his distinguished honored guest and escorted him back upstairs for a small cocktail reception attended by a handful of carefully chosen dignitaries. Then the First Family exchanges pleasantries alone with the other couple (in the case of these photographs, Britain's Prime Minister and Mrs. Harold Wilson).

The hour has come for them to leave and begin the formal part of the evening. Led by a military honor guard bearing the American and presidential flags, the President and Prime Minister, the First Lady and Mrs. Wilson are escorted along a carpeted hallway, past a portrait of Mrs. Ford, and then down the long staircase. The Marine Band strikes up with "Hail to the Chief," signifying the arrival of the President. It is the signal that the evening has begun.

Applause greets the President as he enters the East Room. Then he stands with his wife and guests to begin receiving those who have been awaiting his arrival.

After about half an hour all the guests have passed along the line. The President and Mrs. Wilson turn right, followed by the Prime Minister and Mrs. Ford, and stroll down the 87-foot-long Cross Hall leading from the East Room into the State Dining Room. An honor guard stands at attention, flanking them as they move from one room to the other. The guests follow and proceed to their assigned tables (helped out, if necessary, by other White House aides).

The lights are dimmed, the candles are glowing, and the State Dining Room becomes an intimate setting for animated conversation as the guests dine.

"Most people aren't bashful," Mrs. Ford said, in describing her experience at state dinners during her husband's administration. "They follow the 'switch rule' at first, but after starting out with that etiquette the next thing you know they're talking across the table and having a wonderful time."

By 9:30 P.M. the dinner has been finished and the butlers have removed all the china. It is time for the symbolic exchange of toasts by heads of state. The television floodlights are turned on. The President rises to give his remarks and deliver his toast. Champagne glasses are raised. After the visiting leader offers his own toast, and glasses are raised once more, the formal state dinner is a part of history.

The social evening is not over, however. After the guests have separated, taking with them the menus, matchbooks, and place cards as souvenirs, they gather again in the Red, Green, and Blue rooms for coffee and liqueurs served on silver trays. This is a time for mingling, for exchanging views and information, for chatting with the President or the visiting head of state, for advancing an idea or a political position, or merely for the

167

conviviality of a memorable occasion. Movie stars are seen laughing at a remark by the Secretary of State, corporate magnates talk to politicians, labor leaders to Supreme Court justices, writers to members of the diplomatic corps.

The formal tone of the evening has changed. It is now a time for relaxation, for entertainment and dancing. While the guests are enjoying their after-dinner drinks and coffee, another group is gathering along the Hall, forming a second layer of guests, invited to participate in the last and less formal part of the evening.

At the discretion of the President and his state visitors the after-dinner reception ends, and the guests flock back toward the East Room. While they were dining, the East Room has been transformed again. Gilt chairs stand in semicircular rows facing a platform for the entertainment, which is American.

"I really prefer American entertainment here," Mrs. Ford said. "I would like the world to know we have a little culture, too. My feeling is that if I went to Italy, I wouldn't expect them to show me a cowboy movie. I

would want to hear the best of the Italian artists."

During the entertainment the rest of the White House is still busily at work. The State Dining Room has been sealed off to permit the butlers and workmen to take off the service, dismantle the tables, and begin preparing for the next occasion. A social aide enjoys a brief respite and sits in a chair, awaiting the beginning of the last, and gayest, part of the evening.

The entertainment is finished, and once more the Marine Band, resplendent in red-and-blue uniforms, begins to play in the Cross Hall. Silver trays are brought out again, and champagne is offered. This is the time for all to dance, including the President and the First Lady. White House social aides are encouraged to participate in the dancing, to keep the evening from going flat.

"I dance with anyone who asks me," Mrs. Ford told an interviewer. "My husband does, too. Some of them ask, 'Mr. President, may I have this dance?' and it's all right because we try to keep it as informal as possible."

Protocol requires certain formalities, however. At a designated moment a butler appears at the North Portico carrying the wraps of the state visitors. This is the signal for them to leave. Farewells are taken at the door between the President and his wife and the honored foreign couple. Then they depart.

But the evening is not over, either for the remaining guests or for the White House employees. Especially not the employees. As the dancing continues, often until two o'clock in the morning, the work proceeds in the State Dining Room and in the kitchen. Glasses are removed, tables stripped and carried off, candles extinguished—all while the music

keeps playing. After the last guests have departed, the lights of the White House continue glowing far into the night. The White House is still at work, readying itself for tomorrow, when it must again perform the multiplicity of functions that it has handled so well in the 175 years of its yesterdays.

Into 1976, and on into the American future, the White House endures, working. Home and office for Presidents, house for a nation, even in the most troubled of times it remains a symbol of American promise for the world.

Acknowledgments

This book is the product of one photographer and one reporter, but we would like to acknowledge a larger debt—to all those of our colleagues who over the years have made it possible for the public to gain a better understanding of the working of the White House and of the Presidents who have served there. We only hope the tradition of open access to the people's house, both pictorially and reportorially, will continue.

We would also like to acknowledge the generous cooperation of so many in the White House, from President Gerald R. Ford on down. We owe a special debt to our colleagues at the *Washington Post*, particularly Howard Simons, the managing editor, and Benjamin C. Bradlee, the executive editor. They made it possible for this project to exist.

More personally, this book could not have been produced without the talents and dedication and sheer hard work of Arthur Ellis and David R. Legge of the *Post* and Lois Decker O'Neill of Praeger Publishers. Their imprint is stamped on every page.

Haynes Johnson
Frank Johnston

Washington, D.C.
May 1, 1975

Photo Credits

(Numbers refer to pages.)

Associated Press—17, 27 (center), 35
C. M. Bell (Library of Congress)—31
Matthew Brady (Library of Congress)—10
Ed Clark (Time-Life)—42 (top and bottom)
B. M. Clinedinst (Library of Congress)—29 (bottom left)
Waldon Fawcett (Library of Congress)—27 (top left), 28 (bottom)
Harris & Ewing—27 (bottom), 29 (bottom right)
Rutherford B. Hayes Library—22–23
Frances Benjamin Johnston (Library of Congress)—15, 24, 25, 28 (top), 29 (top),
    37 (bottom)
Library of Congress—title page and pages 13, 21, 27 (top right), 37 (top), 38
Franklin D. Roosevelt Library—41
Mark Shaw—43
United Press International—18, 19, 44
The *Washington Post*—26 (top and bottom), 38 (top and bottom)
Wide World—39

Photos by Frank Johnston begin on page 50.

Photo Equipment

Cameras and accessories used for Frank Johnston's work in this book were manu-
    factured by Leica, Nikon, and Olympus.